THE TERRIER'S VOCATION

PORTRAIT OF THE AUTHOR IN CHARACTERISTIC POSE

THE
TERRIER'S
VOCATION

by

GEOFFREY SPARROW

M.C., T.D., F.R.C.S.

with numerous illustrations by the Author
and copies from old prints

J. A. ALLEN & CO.
LONDON, S.W.1

By the same Author

On Four Fronts with the Royal Naval Division

The Crawley and Horsham Hunt

First published privately 1949.
Second edition, 1961.
First published in this edition 1976.

Published by J. A. Allen & Co., Ltd., 1, Lower Grosvenor Place, Buckingham Palace Road, London, S.W.1 and printed for them in Malta by Interprint (Malta) Ltd.

DEDICATED
TO MY SON
ANTHONY JOHN GUY SPARROW

FOREWORD

★

DURING THE SEASONS 1928-39 I was privileged to manage a Fox-hunting country where Fox-hunting flourished although hardly an acre of the abundant woodlands was "Unkeepered," and where more than half-a-dozen shoots in the country killed between 400 and 500 pheasants on their "First day through." I am proud to record that the 120 keepers and Earth Stoppers who attended my "Keepers' Luncheon and Shoot" in 1939 were so confident in the goodwill existing between Hunting and Shooting that during the Spring 1938, although thirty-one litters of cubs were destroyed by mutual agreement, yet during the ensuing Season hounds killed 78½ brace of foxes.

In this book the Author writes with experience on the subject of terriers and their use, but I would add something from an M.F.H.'s point of view, which no doubt modesty forbids the Author from mentioning. It is not every man who possesses the qualities of tact, geniality and power of command, in order to gain the trust of M.F.H., Covert Owner, and Keeper necessary to become the recognised official Hunt Badger or Fox Digger. There is a serious responsibility resting on the shoulders of such a man, and in the Author I had the right man, bred to the right working strains (as indeed he emphasises that his terriers had to be!) for his father, and grandfather, as well as brother, were all Secretaries of Hunts in their time.

C. GUY CUBITT.

AUTHOR'S PREFACE
TO ORIGINAL EDITION

★

I HAVE ALWAYS wanted to write a book on the Working Terrier, but was prevented for many years by the exacting obligations of general practice and later by the distractions of war. Now that it is all over—or am I mistaken?—I hope to realise my ambition and feel entitled by experience to do so, having worked my terriers in Sussex, Surrey, Hampshire, Devon, Cornwall and Yorkshire and taken over 200 badgers and bolted 49 foxes with them during the last quarter of a century.

By a Working Terrier I mean that "game" sort that will go to ground to Fox, Badger or Otter and keep at him, and I like to judge a dog by his deeds rather than on his appearance only. At one time it was the fashion to have a game-terrier about the place, but of late years he has fallen into comparative obscurity, and it is to revive an interest in him that I have written "The Terrier's Vocation."

My first attempt to tackle it was in the form of four letters to my son and these I wrote, illustrated and gave to him some time since; but as time went on I began to wonder whether this method of approach was outmoded and finding the narrative inadequate, I got down to it with more diligence and expanded and modified it to its present form. A lot of the subject matter comes from my diary which includes about 25 years of terrier work, while part of it was obtained from contemporary and older books which are mentioned in the appendix.

I received much assistance from Lt.-Col. The Hon. C. G. Cubitt, D.S.O., M.F.H., Mr. Sidney Varndell, M.O.H., Miss Varndell and Messrs. John Pasfield, M.R.C.V.S., Charles Denton, H. C. Humphreys, and Arthur Stepney, to whom I offer my sincere thanks. I should also like to thank the Editor of *The Country Sportsman* for permission to publish the drawings and those parts of the text which appeared in that Magazine and the illustration of the Revd. Jack Russell's original terrier 'Trump'. I was very glad to have this, as I had never seen it before and because no book on working terriers is really complete without it. The illustrations have been adapted from various sketches in my diaries and there are a number copied by me from old prints, some of which date back to the fifteenth, sixteenth and seventeenth centuries.

GEOFFREY SPARROW.

AUTHOR'S PREFACE
TO SECOND EDITION

★

TIME always brings change; and, since the war, not by any means for the better. One exception however stands out—the coming of the Foot Followers Clubs, which have been of such assistance to Fox Hunting not only by spreading and fostering its popularity but also by making substantial contributions to the Funds of the Hunt. Many of the members have never had a horse, but they love hound work and like to come out in all weathers to see it, taking a good hard-working terrier with them. This is the cause of the rising popularity of this sort of dog. During the last eighteen months Working Terriers Shows have become the vogue and I judged at two this summer, each of them with well over 100 terriers of various breeds.

I am so often asked for copies of The Terrier's Vocation that a Second Edition is being issued.

GEOFFREY SPARROW.

September, 1960.

CONTENTS

CHAPTER ONE

WE all know the Terrier as an alert, perky little dog, loyal and devoted and bang full of sport, mischief and courage. He makes a good guard and companion but is I think, more suited to the young than to the aged. This is all common knowledge but, as I very much doubt if the public at large are aware of what is the real and proper function of the Terrier, I shall make an attempt to give a picture of it. From the earliest times the Terrier was used to bolt Foxes, work to Badger and Otter and to kill vermin generally, and it was not until the latter half of the last century that the Show Bench came into being and gradually raised a spurious and artificial interest in the dog, and so changed his form and character as to make him well nigh unrecognisable.

To begin with I would lay down the axiom that the BREED is immaterial, but that he must be GAME, and by a game terrier I mean one that will tackle a fox, badger or otter in his earth whether deep or shallow, wet or dry, and keep at him. A good rabbiting terrier, though undoubtedly useful, cannot by virtue of this quality be described as game.

To begin at the beginning, an effort has been made to discover how the Terrier originated, but although it is probably true that he was indigenous to these Islands, there is no consecutive proof of this. In the Book of St. Albans, written in 1406, and the oldest known work on Hunting, Dame Juliana Berners mentions the Terrier in her List of Hounds, and a very curious assortment it is:—

> "Thyse be the names of houndes. Fyrste there is a greyhoun; a Bastard; a Mengrel; a mastif; a Lemor; a Spanyel; Raches; Kenettys; Teroures; Butchers houndes; Dunghyll dogges; Tryndeltaylles; and prycheryd currys; and small lady's popees that bere away the flees and dyvers small sawtes."*

That well-known picture by Brueghel "A Winter Landscape," although the scene is obviously continental gives, I should imagine, a good general impression of some of these dogs. The man in the middle is carrying a dead fox on his shoulder, and here, surely, are "the greyhoun, the Bastard, the Lemor, Butchers' houndes and Teroures." In those days, in many parts of England, men went on foot and were rarely mounted, and usually carried a pole—

---

*A Bastard was a Lurcher.
A Lemor was a Bloodhound.
Raches were Foxhounds.
Kennettys were smaller hounds.
Teroures were Terriers.
Tryndeltaylles were Sheepdogs.

14

as seen in the picture—so as to negotiate the fences and rough places.

Dr. Caius, who founded the College of his name at Cambridge, and was Master of it, found time to write "A Treatisse of Englishe Dogges" (1576) in which he describes the Terrier with great nicety:

> "Another sorte there is which hunteth the Fox and the Badger or Greye onely, whom we call Terrars, because they (after the manner and custome of ferrets in searching for Counyes) creep into the ground, and by that means make afrayde, nyppe and bite the Foxe and the Badger. . . ."

At about the same time "Du Fouilloux" and George Turberville wrote on hunting generally and terriers in particular and they were followed about 100 years later by those two plagiarists Nicholas Cox and Master Blome who copied them almost word for word and contributed very little of real importance or novelty. They all describe the terrier as of two kinds, the one short-legged and smooth, the other long-legged and rough. In "Records of the Old Charlton Hunt" by the Earl of March, 1910, a poem of unknown authorship was found about the year 1737 and the following allusion to the breeding of terriers is contained in it:

> "Let Terriers small be bred, and taught to bay,
> When Foxes find an unstopt Badjers earthe,
> To guide the Delvers, where to sink the Trench;
> Peculiar in their breed, to some unknown,
> Who choose a fighting biting Curr, who lyes
> And is scarce heard, but often kills the Fox;

With such a one, bid him a Beagle join,
The smallest kind, my Nymphs for Hare do use,
That Cross gives Nose, and wisdom to come in
When Foxes earth, and hounds all bayeing stand."

This cross would undoubtedly account for the hound colour of the Fox and Wire terriers and for his nose and tongue.

There is but one more allusion to terriers in this most excellent book: it is to be found among the items of a Bill to the Duke of Richmond:

Novmbr Ye 20 1730.

*paid for digen of a fox at findon	3.	0.
paid for bringn of a teryor hom	1.	6.
paid for dign of a fox at findon	2.	0.

In sporting prints and pictures of the late eighteenth and early nineteenth century a smooth black terrier with tan eyebrows, muzzle and paws was the commonest, but he is hardly seen nowadays, and I suppose remains as the Manchester Terrier.

Everyone has read in "Handley Cross" how John Jorrocks and Charlie Stobbs visited "Slender's" establishment to buy a terrier for the Old Surrey Hunt. I sometimes think we get some of our best working terrier blood from those dogs and the broad cheek and strong jaw of the bull terrier may often be seen in the working terrier of to-day,

It would seem that about 100 years ago there were only three distinct sorts of terrier, the

*To judge by my own experience of the earths round Findon, the price of three shillings is very reasonable, for when I went there—especially to Cissbury—we rarely reached home till after dark!

smooth (Fox) terrier, the rough or wire, and the Scottish; and it is from these that the twenty-one varieties of Terrier recognised by the Kennel Club have been derived.

The first Dog Show in which there was a separate class for fox terriers was in 1862 and in the same year there was another show in which there was a class for "white and other smooth-haired English Terriers, except Black and Tans." Some of the entries for these earlier Shows came from the Oakley, and the Grove and other Hunt Kennels and for some years there can be no doubt that there were some first-class working dogs among them, but as time went on much of the stamina and gameness was lost through lack of use and in-breeding so that in these days it is very doubtful whether, of the 21 different varieties seen on the Show bench, there would be found many dogs that would enter an earth, let alone tackle the occupant. It became the fashion to look down on the working terrier, and the thing is well expressed in Rawdon Lee's book "The Terrier" (1889):

"Time after time has it been stated that the 'Show Dog' is a fraud when he has to earn his living in driving foxes and killing vermin. Possibly he may be so, for an owner with a terrier* worth a couple of hundred pounds is scarcely likely to run any risk with him. In an earth he may be smothered by a fall of soil or crushed by some displacement of rock; and in killing the largest

_____

*To show how the popularity of these dogs has risen in the last 40 years, as high figures as £500 and £1,000 were bid for fox terriers just before the last war.

descriptions of vermin, foulmarts, and the like, his ears may be split and his face torn. If scars on the latter do give an appearance of gameness, they do not enhance his beauty, and after all, the latter goes a long way on the Show bench. A common and less valuable dog will do the work equally well, and if he be killed or maimed, no great loss results to his owner, such as would arise on a champion's destruction."

Well, there it is in a nutshell: personally, I prefer efficiency to beauty if you can't get both—though I'm sure I don't know why not—and I'm glad to think that up to now we don't judge our Surgeons, Generals and Admirals, etc., on their points so much as on their achievements, and long may this be so! But notwithstanding all this, I must confess I rather like the shape of the show-bred smooth Fox Terrier, though I don't care for his long nose and cat feet, but as for the Wire Terrier, no man can tell his shape until he either baths the dog or gets to work with the trimming knife. But it isn't so much the shape as the heart of the dog that matters. I remember when I was a boy, old Higman—huntsman to Squire Coryton of the Dartmoor—expressed the matter in a very happy way. Hounds had marked their fox to ground and there was a lady with a neat looking show bred terrier nearby. She tried the dog and he wouldn't even enter the earth—so she asked Higman "Why he wouldn't go," and Higman replied: "Well ma'm, I suspect e's tu delicate," and a Sussex man expressed it rather differently when he described a reluctant terrier as being "a little duberous." But it's all very well expressing a pious belief, and the fact is that no-one knows if a dog is game unless he tries him, and one or two huntsmen have told me they had had show-bred terriers which were first-class at their work. They had been given away for getting their owners into trouble by killing poultry or cats, and I believe that some years ago some good ones came from the Duchess of Newcastle's strain.

Before leaving the subject, let us take a glance at the present day Sealyham terrier. He is very often too large to enter an earth, his legs are short and deformed and his feet shocking, so that he bears no likeness at all to the original dog, which was small and active, and bred entirely for work.

Of the Bedlington terrier I need say nothing, and merely ask my readers to look at the Show specimen! Some years ago, I met one of the best known breeders of Lakelands, who used to work them with the Blencathra hounds in Cumberland and judged the classes of them for the first years after the recognition of the breed by the Kennel Club, and he told me that when it got to the point that he didn't know where the Lakelands ended and the Welshmen began, he thought it was time to stop. In 25 years I have only seen four or five Show terriers that were game, and only one of these was first-class. I know that among the Border terriers there are still some game ones of the Show Class, tho' why I cannot tell—but the Fancy do not appear to have spoilt them entirely yet, nor changed their shape and character as in most breeds.   A look at the picture of the old Earth Stopper (1767) will show that the darker of his two terriers is very similar to the Border of to-day, and this type is frequently to be seen working to fox, otter and badger.

N. Drake, pinxit

ARTHUR WENTWORTH, OF BULMER NEAR CASTLE
HOWARD, YORKS. AETAT 75. 1767

CHAPTER TWO

GETTING A PACK TOGETHER—CHOICE OF TYPE—
BREEDING—MANAGEMENT

No-one can tell a game terrier by looking at him (though a prominent dark eye is a help) and a trial to ground is the only "acid fast" test. Just because a dog is bad tempered and quarrelsome is no guarantee that

THE QUARRELSOME SORT

he will go to ground, for everyone knows he is a nuisance, and it has been proved time and again that such dogs are by no means invariably game. I had a dog called Patch that luckily proved an exception: he was the sort that would go for any man or dog that went near him, but he was so good at his work that I could overlook it, and he was only like it on the day.

I used to tie him up far down in the wood and warn all and sundry not to go near him, but I need scarcely say that this warning was almost invariably ignored.

Presently some luckless swain would wander in the dog's vicinity, when a hoarse cry and the rending of cloth would be heard, but never a sound from old Patch, who had taken hold at once, without warning. I remember such a man coming up to me with an area of pink bottom peeping through a large rent in his pants. To his question: "What about my trousers then?" I thought it best to tell him that he needed a tailor more than a doctor and to apply iodine to the injured part combined with a denial of all responsibility. I must say that he took it very well, and most fellows that enjoy a day's sport are the same. Working to the adage that "one can't make omelettes without breaking eggs," it will be abundantly clear that a half dozen good terriers are needed during the course of the season, exclusive of un-entered dogs: even then, anyone with a good hard terrier will be welcome. Terriers may be laid up for a few weeks as it is never wise to work a dog before his wounds are soundly healed.

It is best to buy a puppy from a known breeder of working terriers, and one who works them himself. I rarely buy an entered dog, as there is nearly always something wrong with him, or why is the owner so anxious to part? A proper price for a puppy is usually five pounds, and for an entered dog, a tenner or even more, and it is most essential to see him worked or to have him on trial. The breed of terrier is not important, and a man can please his fancy—I have used

PARSON JACK RUSSELL'S ORIGINAL TERRIER 'TRUMP'

Fox—Wire—Sealyhams, Borders, Lakelands and Jack Russells,* and they are all good if bred right—it's the STRAIN that counts. I was never very particular what my dogs looked like, indeed, they only had about one face between any two of them, and I have no objection to crossing different kinds if it is done with care and it gets some rare sorts. I had a Border—Jack Russell

*Frequent references are made to the Jack Russell Terrier in here and elsewhere. By this I mean a white terrier, black or tan markings, a little 'up on the leg' and with good shoulder. I am pretty sure the Parson never established a definite breed, but liked his terriers to run on with hounds. A description may be found in the Appendix.

cross at one time that was as good as any I ever saw; but then she had a working pedigree back to the nineties on both sides. The real blood must be there or the pups are sure to throw back to soft lines. The sire should be from two to five years old and no more, or he may get a litter of nervy little runts! It is as well not to work him too hard at the time, for he cannot get good stuff if he is continually convalescing from wounds.

Some people object to the black and tan and blue varieties, as they are apt to be chopped by hounds, or hit with a spade. This is true enough and I know of such casualties, but my two Lakelands and the Border Terrier never gave any trouble. If I was asked to choose my own stamp of terrier I would have a smooth dog, weighing from twelve to sixteen pounds, with a strong jaw—not snipey like the show breeds—a good back, neck and shoulders, and fairly long legs.

THE RIGHT SORT

The length doesn't matter. They can be folded up while bad shoulders cannot. He must have plenty of heart room, and throw his tongue well when up to his game. Lakelands are usually rather long in the leg, for when they go to ground in the Screes on the mountainside they may jump down off a ledge and be unable to get back if low to the ground. At the end of last season two Ullswater Hunt Terriers were trapped in this way and only got out with the greatest difficulty. The size and weight of dog depends upon the use for which he is intended; for Fox and Otter from twelve to sixteen pounds, and for Badger up to twenty. These weights are only approximate, and quite large terriers can get into small holes if they want to, though there is always the risk of getting jammed.

Nervous, snappy types are quite unsuitable for breeding, and should never be used. If the dog is on the large side, he should be mated to a small bitch and vice versa. Some people advise a cross of Staffordshire Bull Terrier every ten generations to maintain the strength of jaw and stamina, and if the pups are rather large, mate them in turn to smaller terriers. I believe it works well, but have not seen any of this breeding, and in any case the ordinary methods give good results.

Rough or broken coated terriers are got by crossing a Jack Russell or Sealyham with a smooth one, and real rough ones from a Jack Russell and Sealyham cross. Personally, I don't like these, as they get so dirty and wet, and one cannot see and treat wounds so well.

The brood-bitch selected should be in sound health and of strong constitution, with normal heat periods, that is six monthly intervals and three weeks of heat. Conception is most favourable at the twelfth day, but persists to the end. It was formerly considered that Blackberry litters or those born in the Autumn would never thrive, but the use of Cod Liver Oil makes it of no matter when they are born.

Half-way through gestation, violent exercise should be replaced by routine work in strict moderation, and this may be carried on to full term. It is also the best opportunity to clear the bitch of Tapeworm* and to attend to skin trouble such as fleas, lice, or mange, if found.

At one week before full term, the hair should be clipped from the bearing and inner buttocks, and this area and the teats washed with soap and warm water, to prevent the spread of Round Worm from dam to pups.

The bitch should now be accustomed to her whelping box, which should consist of three plain boards laid together to make a platform sufficiently roomy for her to stretch at full length, raised three inches from floor level, and provided with a wooden lip on the outer side, three inches high. The bedding should be

---

*For tapeworm use the new alkaline salt of Asetarsol (Tenoban, Nemural, etc.) which does not require starvation, and which should invariably be followed in twenty minutes by a soapy enema.

wood wool, or failing this, clean trussed wheat or oat straw.

Bitches are sometimes rather particular and choose funny places to whelp in. Some years ago, a foxhound bitch of the Linlithgow and Stirling dug a hole in the brick floor, and I had a Seluki bitch that did the same in Sinai during the late war.

Three days before term, the diet must be changed to soft food with milk, and a dose of Liquid Paraffin, and the udders and bearing washed again.

The period of gestation is usually 63 days; whelps born before the 57th day rarely survive.

Whelping in maiden bitches is frequently accompanied by restlessness for as much as 48 hours before commencement. Such animals should always be given plenty of time to settle. The act of labour is slowly rhythmical, associated with real straining, and sometimes accompanied by deep groans, but older bitches frequently produce their litter with little or no preliminaries. In any case, the first whelp should have arrived by two hours after the onset of real labour. The interval between puppies is most irregular, sometimes extending to a whole day, but the arrival of the last-born is followed by obvious relief on the part of the dam, who now gives her undivided attention to cleaning the pups. Whelping should have been carried out on sheets of plain newspaper, which can be burned and replaced as frequently as necessary. This is now replaced by wood wool.

The bitch's diet should consist of soft milky foods with a dose of one dessert-spoon of liquid paraffin, for the next three days, and on the fourth day the puppies' tails and dew claws should receive attention. The dock should not be too short—it will be all there is to catch hold of when the dog grows up. Some prefer their dogs undocked but I do not, and consider it very unsightly except in Scottish, Border or Bedlington Terriers. The bitch should now have regular exercise and three normal meals a day.

At the fourth week the puppies' teeth begin to pierce the gums, and weaning is generally commenced in the fifth week, at which time it is normal for the bitch to vomit predigested food and this should not be cleared away; the puppies should be allowed to eat it. They should be fed thrice daily on lactol, milk puddings, well boiled porridge and minced boiled tripe. As time goes on, more solids are added and in the eighth week four meals are given, and the bitch removed entirely. This is the time to worm* the puppies.

It may so happen that the dam, after a successful parturition, either fails to produce an adequate milk supply or dies from some puerperal complication. In this case a foster mother will be required and these are hard to get, and costly at short notice. Age difference in the litters is an objection, but first week puppies have before now been put to a foster parent whose

*Chenopodium Castor Oil should be given after eighteen hours fasting. Or Ruby.

litter was already weaned. Unless arrangements can be made beforehand, one may have to accept what he can get, but a bad-tempered bitch should be rejected if possible.

The process of adoption is not usually difficult; it is best to separate the foster mother from her pups for four hours, so that the breasts are full. and then put the new puppies to her, and she will be glad of the relief. Some people advise wiping a little broth on them, so that the bitch will begin by licking them.

Kennels should be double walled—of corrugated iron outside and wood lined—and facing south. They should be light and airy, yet draught proof and with a small exercise yard. The wire between runs must be fine mesh for nothing is worse than a fight through the netting and one or other combatant is sure to get a foot through and be bitten. Bitches in season and quarrelsome dogs should be kept separate; if not there will be trouble and moreover they will bark all night. I found all this very troublesome when I lived in the middle of a town and especially at full moon, when I was not at all popular with my neighbours.

Any dog that falls sick must be removed at once, and the Kennel disinfected. Some terriers love to gnaw the woodwork and they are very destructive, but treating it with Jeyes Fluid will soon stop that.

Terriers require plenty of exercise and good food once a day, which should be solid and not all a'wash, as this does them little good. Raw meat and oatmeal should be the basis when obtainable. In the hot weather it is best to cook the meat and for greenstuff I prefer spinach and young nettles well boiled. Dogs should always be allowed to eat grass which is a good alterative, and they should be, if anything, a little on the thin side for a fat one is good for nothing and cannot stand up to hard work. I always give them meat bones, other than rabbit* or chicken, though some vets disagree with this.

It is a good thing to use a flea powder once a week as a routine and if a dog becomes lousy he should be washed, rubbed down and dusted with a louse powder.

---

*This applies to small dogs; I always give my lurcher rabbit boiled with the skin, bones and all.

CHAPTER THREE

EARLY TRAINING—RAT CATCHING—
CUB HUNTING—THE SOUND OF THE HORN—
THE TERRIER MAN

WHETHER a puppy be bought or home bred, his owner should undertake the training himself and let no irresponsible person fool about with him, though there is no objection to putting a puppy or two to walk with a Game Keeper or sporting farmer if he is taken back at about 12 months. His education will depend on his size and how forward he is, but in every case he should be entered to rats first, as there is nothing makes a dog quicker or handier; but not until he has his permanent dentition.

Some rats must be caught and shown to him to make him keen, and then shaken down into a loose box one at a time so that he can have a go.

The best way to catch them is to put down a little corn where they trade and then a roll of wire netting while continuing to feed them there. Presently they will get used to the wire and when it is replaced by the trap suitably baited, they will be caught readily enough. The best way to get a dog to work in the dark is to shake a rat into two or three pipes laid end to end and with one extremity closed: then let the young dog follow the rat and kill him there. A terrier should be taught at an early stage to use his nose and there is no better way than to take him to the fields and hedgerows after the corn is cut for it is here that rats concentrate before going into the buildings in the cold weather. A spade or light grafter is the best tool to take, for presently one of the terriers will mark a rat to ground and he should not be interfered with, for it teaches him to work and he may speak to it. It is a mistake to let two terriers work at the same hole for the older dog will push the young 'un away or they may fight. Presently one should dig over the dog as it makes him used to the spade and to earth falling about him. He will soon give information when close at the rat for he will keep diving at the hole. While digging here, other holes should be stopped for any rats that bolt are not likely to be seen again.

It is always worth while to draw barns, stables, forage sheds and henhouses, particularly in the cold weather and rats are sometimes caught if the terrier is brought up quietly and released as soon as the door is open. One may have to pull up the flooring of a hen house as rats always go underneath, or tilt it if not too heavy. To catch rats in permanent buildings

NABBED HIM QUICK

one must find the hole or grating through which they enter and endeavour to make a small trap door that will let down over them from outside by a string. As soon as ever this has been done the dog must be let in at once.

Threshing a stack is great fun and there is always plenty of demand for a good terrier. It is, I believe, compulsory to have wire netting round in order to prevent any rats escaping. Sometimes there are plenty of rats, at other times but few. The longer the delay before the thresher comes the fewer the rats as I suppose they find less to eat there. At the beginning they bolt by ones and twos which are readily accounted for, but the majority like to remain till the end and when the stack is reduced to about a foot or eighteen inches high the fun really begins. We killed 70 to one terrier some years ago. The only trouble is there is always a battalion of men armed with sticks, each one of whom is likely to hit the terrier. These should be persuaded to operate outside the wire while the dogs work within.

Of course, ferreting is the most entertaining method, and it always pays to have a dog or two entered to ferrets. Let the owner take a young dog with him whenever he feeds them, and never so much as let him look at the ferret and chide him if he does so. Ferrets should be handled as much as possible and one allowed to run along in front of the dog, not letting the latter move near him, and in this way each will get to know the other. Some people think it a good thing if a ferret bites a puppy; this is quite wrong, as their mutual attitude should be co-operative and friendly, and besides, the terrier may turn on the ferret and kill it.

When a young dog has been broken to ferrets above ground, they should be worked together. He should be kept on the lead at first, made to sit back and wait for the rat to bolt and then immediately released. Later when the ferret comes up to the mouth of the hole any attempt to go forward should be stopped at once by a tap on the nose. It sounds a nasty kind of rebuke but is really only a mild reminder. A dog should never work at a hole while the ferret is in the earth as he may get bitten and then will most surely kill it. A white ferret should be used at first as polecat ferrets are dark and may be mistaken for a rat until the dog is used to them.

Rats can be bolted by stinking them out with exhaust gas from a car, but I do not like the method, as the dogs may get carbon monoxide poisoning which is often fatal. Messrs. S. Young & Son Ltd., of Misterton, Somerset, used to make a gassing machine and turn out the cartridges too.

It is a curious fact that foxes have been known to bolt if a ferret enters the earth.

Since the greatest danger to dogs of this type is infection with leptospiral jaundice, they should be protectively vaccinated against the condition. Rats are the carriers of this disease, which frequently proves fatal. Unvaccinated dogs which develop indefinite symptoms two or three days after being rat-bitten should receive serum as quickly as possible.

A dog should never be allowed to chase cats; for if he kills one—which he will, sooner or later—the resultant reaction will be enough to cause "alarm and despondency": a vast number of proprietors or part owners will turn up, as if by magic, and all in full cry: while the man and his dog will have to beat a hasty retreat and maintain the maximum morale consistent with such an undignified manoeuvre. It will be rather like what the Devil said when they plucked the pig: "A Hell of a row and no wool!"

EVICTING THE TENANT

As a general rule eighteen months to two years is the right age to enter a young 'un to bigger stuff, but to begin with he must not be confronted with anything very formidable. He should be taken cub-hunting* and if his owner is invited

*The cub-hunting season begins as soon as the corn is cut, say August-September, and usually gives way to the Hunting Season proper about the first Saturday in November. The dates are decided by the M.F.H.

to try him to a cub, he will not be overfaced. It is a mistake to let anyone else enter him and there should be as little noise as possible at the time.

I think it takes more patience and care to enter a Border terrier than any other kind. He is usually of high courage, but naturally shy and nervous at the least noise, and thus he may be very readily spoiled: and the same may be said of all terriers to a lesser degree.

Some years ago there was a wire haired dog called Trueman at the Crawley and Horsham Kennels which was one of the best I ever saw; he had rather a shy way with him and couldn't abide a lot of raucous halloaing, nor would he enter a hole unless he wanted to. The first time I saw him at work out hunting, they couldn't get him to go at all and were just going to give it up when someone said: "There's a heck of a noise underneath where I'm standing.' Well, it was quite obvious he had waited his time and then gone into another hole, got up to his fox and was busy at him. At the beginning he looked abject, mean and utterly lacking in courage, showing how deceptive a dog may be.

Before putting a dog into the earth it is wise to see if the hole is large enough for his reception and not half full of rubble, in which case it should be cleared and at the same time a level approach made for the dog to stand on, for dogs—especially when young and untried—do not like going down hill to a hole full of earth or rubble and with Charlie or Brock just round the corner.

When the dog has entered the hole and gone from view, the less said the better: to huick and to holloa or indeed play on the flute, does naught but confuse him. When he has settled and begun barking, he is very probably up to his game and may be cheered unless there is any doubt, when it pays to wait. In "dog language" the same words must always be used for the same things, remembering that speech is silver while silence is golden. To keep on "eagering" a dog is most unwise, and is likely to make a fool of him for he will bark at a tin can if one goes on long enough, and I have known a dog go just inside the hole and bark at nothing! It must be remembered that the noise and the crowd are quite new to a young dog and one must make allowances, and have plenty of patience for he won't have a clue to what it is all about, unless he can actually see the Fox or Badger in the mouth of the hole. If he won't go, it is a good plan to try an old dog to show him the way and let the young 'un follow him or go in later.

As time goes on and one manages to collect or breed a few good terriers he should try and specialise, using a small dog with a good nose to find, another, perhaps not so good, to carry on for a while and—in Badger digging—a strong hard dog to "bag up" with, for when the Badger is facing one, it is a great comfort to have a

"Caesar" dog handy. If a dog is very small he may make a good "pipe cleaner" and such are very valuable and scarce, for foxes, and particularly cubs, can enter an earth or drain that an ordinary dog cannot negotiate, and indeed may be considered capable of entering any place where they can put their head. A dog that will work to a "stop" or pile of earth left by a Badger behind him as he digs on, is a treasure and should never be used for rough work if avoidable.

I do not advise using terriers for rabbiting or coursing, as this quarry should be most carefully avoided, and it looks rather daft to ask half a dozen stalwarts to remove nearly a ton of earth for one to take out a Jack Rabbit! Of course it's grand fun, and terriers will draw a gorse covert as well as or better than a spaniel. I had a Sealyham at one time that would find and retrieve birds and ground game, but the best plan is to keep separate dogs for this work.

Hunt terriers are carried in various ways; some Hunts have a mounted man, others go on bike or foot and they have to be very wiry and active as some of them are past middle age.

Terriers ran with hounds at one time, but they are very apt to riot, and may go to ground in a big place and no-one the wiser, so the practice has been discontinued.

In the thirties Rex Smith, aged eighty-three, was still going strong in the South Oxfordshire country, and said to be "as fresh as a two-year-old." He had followed on foot for fifty-three years and for forty of these had taken the Hunt Terriers.

Harry Tester of the Southdown owns to sixty-seven I believe, and can go almost incredible distances, never being far away when wanted.

One should get to know the sound of the horn and what the various calls mean: blowing to ground, and when they want a terrier are specially important, though it's not always easy to tell, especially at a distance.

THE MOUNTED TERRIER MAN *see page* 39

For a fox to ground: if to dig—the call is

Since the war, establishments have been drastically cut down and terriers are often left in a cottage near the meet or given to someone in a car, and in most countries there are sportsmen interested in working terriers who will follow hounds on the chance of getting their dogs to ground.

I remember some years ago our old master was trying to find out whether a man who had been seen nearby with a dog was the man he was looking for and he asked a countrified sort of chap what sort of fellow he had seen and he replied: "He had a face like a bag o' lard!" and this was such a graphic description, he knew his man at once.

After the opening meet in early November, it may be necessary to bolt a fox—some are "bespoke" poultry killers, live in a drain or earth hard by and never run a yard when hunted—but seldom attractive to anyone with a good horse. The weather is usually chill and unkind and the wind keen, especially on the exposed side of a bleak hill, and men, horses and hounds are soon perished with cold, so that no-one but the terrier man and his dogs enjoy it. I think the runner has a lot of fun, and in big woodlands sees as much and sometimes

THE MAN WITH A FACE LIKE A BAG OF LARD *see p.* 41

more than the field. Before I could afford a horse I would often follow with a terrier and sometimes took one on my country rounds on the chance of seeing hounds: I remember on one occasion I was able to bolt a fox for them and continue my round later, and I know that during those few years I had a lot of fun and practically no expense!

42

There was another occasion, however, when I did not enjoy myself and I'm not likely to forget it though it's more than twenty years ago now. Hounds ran a fox to ground in Bigginholt near Storrington late one afternoon, and I put in a Lakeland terrier called Bing and away he went. Nothing more was heard of him and at 5 o'clock hounds went home and there I was! I left at nightfall and came next morning at 6 and dug him out. There was a lot of earth behind him and he had been trying to get at his fox but was rather too large for the job and it proved a lesson to me.

Some people will wipe a little aniseed round the edges of the tube, so when Charlie is bolted he will carry a very high scent. This is a very unsportsmanlike thing and, I believe and hope, comparatively rare.

CHAPTER FOUR

THE FOX, THE BADGER AND THE OTTER AND THE
HUNTING OF THEM, WITH SPECIAL
REFERENCE TO THE TERRIER

BEFORE hunting an animal, it seems to me most important to know something of its appearance and habits, and so I think a description of the Badger, Fox and Otter will not be out of place.

They are all carnivorous; for whatever may be said of the belief that the Badger lives entirely on roots and beetles, one thing is certain, God never gave an animal such a dentition to that end. The question of whether he kills lambs is of course another matter, and not very clearly proven. His chief flesh diet is young rabbits, and sometimes poultry or young pheasants. He is more especially the enemy of the keeper who is trying to bring on hand-reared birds. He will enter the rearing field at night and with his leathery upturned nose upset the coop and take foster mother, poults and all. It was with this knowledge that, some years ago, I presented a sow badger and two pigs to a man who did not preserve foxes (a vulpicide), tho' his family hunted. We shook 'em down into the main earth during the night, and he none the wiser. What a party we made—there was old "Busy" with the sack full of badgers, two ladies, the groom and myself with a torch which I seldom dared

THE BADGER AT HOME

to shine—as we stumbled up through the heather and bracken to the main earth under the Scotch firs. I am sure "Busy" was glad to be relieved of his burden as we put the neck of the bag into the hole and let the occupants disappear into the bowels of the earth. I was glad too, to reach home as I did not think we should have looked our best if discovered. I am a great believer in "doing good by stealth" as was said in the Bible, or "let not your right hand know what your left is doing"; curiously enough, altho' I cannot imagine who gave the game away, the matter was well-known in the district. I became aware of this while digging a badger near there some two or three years later: I was lying with my head in the hole listening to the terrier tackling his opponent and looked up at an old chap standing above me and said: "There's someone at home, tho' I don't know who," and he replied: "You know well enough Doctor." On asking him what he meant, he said: "Well, you put him there," and no amount of denial on my part could convince him to the contrary.

Another habit of the Badger, is to bore great holes in the rabbit wire round cornfields and this is a source of great annoyance to the farmers.

Before going any further, I should like to make it clear that, personally, I like Bill Brock well enough: he's a good fellow and interferes with nobody—I wish everyone was like him—if nobody interferes with him. If roused however, he is a most formidable opponent as many a

46

terrier could testify if endowed with the power of speech. But there can be no doubt that when he becomes too numerous and especially if rabbits are scarce, he takes poultry and moreover makes the country so hollow that stopping is well nigh impossible and sport much interfered with. I am no great advocate for killing him, but think he should be shaken down elsewhere— as I said before—or "moved on" as the police have it. When shaking him down, fifteen miles is the minimum distance and I believe they come back even then. I feel very strongly that

THE OLDEST BRITON *see page* 48

47

the Badger should receive the respect due to him as our oldest Briton: he is no interloper or mushroom toff, but rather a country character like the rabbit catcher and he was here long before the Romans.

The Badger belongs to the Mustelidae — among which are the Otters, Stoats, Weazels, Martens and Ferrets—called so because of an anal gland which is common to them, and which excretes a pungent substance on any excitement or danger. The old theory that the Badger belonged to the Bear family is quite erroneous and has long been abandoned. His appearance and marking—alternating black and white bars on the face and the greyish appearance of back and sides, with a black or dark brown belly— are familiar to most people. Albinoism is rare but known—there is a stuffed one in the Brighton Museum and some years ago one was killed at Machynlleth which was clearly an albino. It was reported (by Hastings Smith of Aberystwyth, Cards.) as "of a reddish fawn colour. The broad stripes on the sides of the head, usually black, were of golden fawn." No mention was made of the eyes which I suspect were pink.

On the South Downs Badgers are usually Black and Silvery-White, while in the Weald they are much browner in tone, and even the white on the face is of a sallow colour. I have always thought the Downland Badger was more active than his brother of the Weald.

The Badger possesses five toes, has a peculiar

dentition, and the mandible or lower jaw works as a hinge. It does not move so freely as in most skulls; but just opens and shuts like a door.

He is found all over the Temperate Zone, in N. America, Europe, Asia and even in Palestine. Being of a retiring disposition, he prefers to live in an unfrequented wood or copse, though this is not always the case as I have seen one or two settes quite close to dwelling houses or to much frequented pathways and some years ago we dug a 34½ lb. Badger from a sette which extended for forty feet round three sides of a swimming pool at St. George's School, Weybridge, and threatened to demolish it. I believe they have him set up there in the Museum. Very often his earth or sette is in a bank above a stream, tho' on the South Downs it may be at some considerable distance from water. He is believed to hibernate or lie up in the winter, and live on his fat; and I believe he generally does so, at least for some of the time, tho' I have more than once seen hounds find and kill one above ground in the hunting season. I rather think it depends on the weather and, as in late years we have generally had our Summer weather during the Winter, Brock is encouraged to come out and enjoy it.

He is a most skilful miner and sapper, and digs for himself a formidable redoubt, sometimes consisting of as many as three different storeys, and possessed of a big shaft to bring in air from above. So good a workman is he with

49

his five-toed foot that he digs as fast as a man with a spade. It is fairly easy to estimate the size of his establishment by the amount of earth which is piled up outside the various holes. The sette is kept scrupulously clean, and they say that badgers prevent mange in a country by keeping the earth spotless and tidy. This is very likely true, because badgers and foxes are frequently found in the same earth, and sometimes take over from each other: but if there is offal, such as the head of a cockerel, or lamb bones, or a dead rat on an earth, you may be sure there is no badger in it, at least in that end of it. Of course a Fox cannot oust a Badger from his home by force of arms, but I believe he causes him to quit in disgust at the untidy and squalid conditions of co-habitation.

Leading to and from the sette are regular tracks thro' the undergrowth as Brock always uses the same paths; this is called "trade" and should always be carefully examined to determine if an earth is occupied or not. At one or other end of the sette is usually a small hole where he leaves his billet; as the badger is very hygienic altho' he only has "outside sanitation." Another of his house-keeping habits is to air his bedding at the mouth of the sette. In the same earth, though in different parts of it, may be found foxes, rabbits and even rats, all seeming to have some kind of understanding or *modus vivendi*.

The badger stays at home during daylight,

usually leaving his sette at 10 or 11 p.m., and returning before dawn. This is the time he supplies his larder and visits the neighbouring warrens and hen-runs. I rather think he takes eggs as well, because I once found a golf ball well inside an earth on the Mannings Heath Golf Course. I suppose Brock had mistaken it for an egg. Foxes and Badgers both like to be home before dawn, and it is for this reason that a good keeper does his stopping before 6 a.m. in the winter. The keeper of today tends to stroll along after breakfast and thereby, I am convinced, often stops in his fox. It is a long job to "put to"* a badger sette, and unless it is done very thoroughly with logs and tree branches, old Brock will have it open again or ever hounds come, and the huntsman will be as angry as the keeper is surprised when a fox goes to ground almost as soon as found.

Unfortunately since the 2nd Great War there are practically no keepers and therefore no stopping worth the name.

Badgers are clumsy beggars and are quite frequently run over at night or electrocuted on the line—this seldom happens to Charlie!

The Fox is carnivorous and belongs to the Canidae or dogs, but curiously enough a dog-fox cross is an impossibility, and I think it is agreed by all observers that it has never happened. He weighs from 12½ to 20 lbs. and like

---

*To "put to" means to stop an earth.

the dog has four toes. He goes clicketting in the winter and the vixen usually has her four or five cubs in March. She does not as a general rule draw out a deep earth, tho' she may take over a Badger's sette or a deep place in a clitter of rocks or the screes on a mountain side. The earth may be quite shallow in a wood or hedgerow or anywhere that's dry. In the Holderness Country a woodstack is frequently used and there are a number of them; she may even have her cubs in a hollow tree. By a curious dispensation of providence she carries little scent while in cub.

When six or seven weeks old the cubs come to the mouth of the earth and at three months the vixen moves them so that they can hunt for themselves. It is while they are helpless that she does the most damage. A fox's staple diet is rabbits, frogs, beetles and rats, and scarcity of these drives her, particularly at this time, to the hen runs, where she is an indiscriminate killer.

In some parts she seeks no earth at all and drops her cubs in a hedgerow above ground. Such foxes are called stub breed. The foxes round Rusper in the Crawley and Horsham country are of this kind for the most part, and I have never seen, and only once heard of, a fox run to ground there.

Before the last war I used to visit all the earths in my vicinity in the Spring of the year in order to find out who was at home. Sometimes an earth would be unoccupied, at other times, lying hidden and quite silent in the bushes nearby, I would see a litter of cubs come out to romp and play at the entrance, and what a lovely sight they were!

I never saw Bill Brock and I very much doubt if he comes out at high noon: he's a somnolent, lazy chap and prefers the cool and solitude of the night and it means a sit of many a long hour down-wind of the earth, in complete silence and without even a whiff of tobacco, before there's even a remote chance of seeing him.

Fox cubs are much more lively and inquisitive. They have often been known to come out and have a look, even when someone is digging down to remove the litter. And, of course, if taken young they get very tame and make good pets to anyone who doesn't mind the smell; but at all times they are more timid and distrustful than a Badger and Otter as pets.

During a hunt a fox may run over an earth or pass through a drain or culvert and not dwell there, and when a hound or terrier marks, he will be false. In the same way a terrier will sometimes speak in a sette when there is nothing but the bedding there. It all goes to prove that to be really first-class a terrier must have a very delicate sense of smell—he must have NOSE.

It's sometimes hard to find a fox, especially after a wet and windy night when foxes will lay to ground and a huntsman may draw for hours with never a touch, though some have an

A MOORLAND FOX

54

uncanny knack of knowing just where to go. In some countries there are artificial earths whence a fox can be bolted readily and this may be sound enough, but I think there is more to be said against than for it as foxes in such quarters are very accessible to unscrupulous persons. There is no doubt they like quiet and warmth and a good gorse or whin cover is as likely a place to hold as any, but any rough warm brake or thick hedgerow is worth drawing. On Dartmoor hounds frequently find drawing over the open moor, and if it is fine and warm Charlie may be asleep in the sun. I've seen a fox poked out of an elm tree before now quite ten feet from the ground and they are frequently found in pollarded willows, or at the end of a lake or pond where they lie warm and dry on the moss hags among the alders and they will sometimes lie along the branches of big rhododendrons. A good covert must have some holding; it is no use if it's all bare between the trees. Of late years tree felling and clearing has spoilt many a good place, and in many parts of the country foxes are scarce and the more so as there is a gunner in almost every field!

Foxes in different parts of the country vary a good deal in size and stoutness, though I am sure they are all of the same variety. The moorland, mountain and some forest foxes are bigger than those seen in the vale and are often referred to in writings as greyhound foxes, being a sort of mauvish-grey and very large. I have the mask of a Dartmoor fox by me here, which is about the size of the head of a Collie dog.

The other sort of fox is usually more reddish in colour and in many cases the original stock has been imported from France or Norway. In the Crawley and Horsham Country a number were imported just after the mange epidemic had almost cleared the country; I believe it was the year—curiously enough—the Derby was won by Flying Fox. At all events the story goes that the man who shook 'em down said to his friends: "There's a tip for you, my lads."

I have never heard of Albinoism in foxes, tho' I bolted one with a white pad on one occasion.

A fox is often referred to as "Charlie," called so after Charles James Fox, a crafty politician in the days of George III: in some country districts he is known as "Master Reynolds," while in Scotland "Tod" is the name often used. And speaking of "crafty" reminds me that the old theory that a fox will sham dead is perfectly true and I have seen it happen. I had been left to dig a fox while hounds were on to another and after a time we came on our terrier up to his fox which was apparently lifeless, lying on his side with eyes shut and tongue out, and you could have picked him up. Well, I took the terrier away, put a spade over the hole and waited for them to come back. When we took the spade away, Charlie had gone back into the earth and we had to work for quite a while before we bolted him.

A fox may be hunted into a neighbouring country but may neither be dug nor bolted with a terrier. A misunderstanding on this point led to a duel between Col. Jolliffe and Mr. Maberley of the Old Surrey about a hundred years ago: but in those days people took things more seriously than they do now.

In January and February, when foxes go clicketting, hounds sometimes find one that is ten or twelve miles from his home and these are the times for the best gallops ever.

The Otter belongs to the Mustelidae, is as much at home in the water as on land, and lives on fish, frogs, eels, slugs, moorhens and occasional rabbits and poultry. She is more or less a fox on dry land, though she has no regular home and is more of a vagrant like the "gypo." She usually comes out at sundown and will not return to her holt from hunting until just before dawn: during that time she may travel anything up to fifteen or twenty miles. She does not hibernate like the Badger but in the winter may go down to the Marshes or the coast, or if it is very cold she may move to the head of the river where the springs are not frozen over; she will sometimes kill a fish out of pure fun, take one bite out of the shoulder and leave it; so as a general rule she is not popular with fishermen or water bailiffs. She is, however, full of wiles and tends to avoid traps, while her thick coat is very resistant to pellets.

The distribution is the same as the Badger,

THE OTTER

and I am almost sure otters are found in Syria and Palestine, for the Barada River and the upper reaches of the Jordan are ideal, and once I saw an otter's pelt for sale in the streets of Damascus.

Otters weigh from 18-26 lbs. (male) and from 13-22 lbs. (female) tho' they have been recorded at 40 lbs. They have a litter of four to five cubs at almost any time of the year.

Otters, when working up stream, will cut a corner and go overland; it is at such places if the banks are sandy or muddy that one should look for his pad mark or sele.

His length of stay on a river will depend on the supply of fish and freedom from disturbance; but sooner or later he will go down to the sea to clean his coat from lice. Later he may return or work his way along the coast to another estuary. It is the fishermen that see most of the otter in his natural surroundings and occupations.

The Otter hunting season is from April to October. Some people will tell you it is slow and will talk of "love and lunch," but those who like Hound work and a beautiful riverside scenery, will get them at their best. Is there anything better than the sight of a pack of otter hounds crossing a river in full cry?

This sort of hunting may be seen at its best where the rivers have a shingly bottom so that the water runs clear and is not so readily churned up into a kind of pea soup, as in the southern or eastern counties. But my only complaint with it is that you may be left about ten or twelve miles to hike home at the end of a hard day.

The Fox-hound is as good as the Otter-hound for this sport, and most packs have a number of them; he swims as well and has more drive. The Otter-hound is too low scented and may dwell on a drag anything up to 48 hours old. He is said to go back to the old Southern Hound, a heavy, coarse-throated, long-eared, low scented dog with a very deep note. A few of the Crowhurst Otter-hounds have a cross of Dumfries Fox-hound, which has a cross of Blood-hound.

Otters have been hunted with terriers, but it is difficult to get them entered and the same may be said of hounds, for Parson Jack Russell did 3,000 miles of river without finding an otter, nor did he do so until someone gave him an entered hound. It is essential to have at least one hound that will mark at a holt. Otherwise you may draw over him and have much work for nothing.

Otters may lie up in a holt or "lie rough" elsewhere, and they are occasionally found on a collection of flotsam on the water. Their holt is very usually under tree roots overhanging the water, at other times among rocks or perhaps behind the brick or stone work of a weir or bridge. A good and experienced huntsman will be familiar with most of such places in his country. When an otter is put down* on a

---

*An otter is said to be "put down" when found.

biggish water, it is sometimes advisable to make a stickle or chain of people across the stream to prevent him going up or down as the case may be. Fifty years ago they used to use a thirty foot net which was held up by the followers, but it is never seen now.

An otter when hunted will go to ground if and when he can and in rivers where there are a lot of rocks and boulders, it is not always easy to bolt him. I remember the Dartmoor Otter Hounds coming to Cornwall for a few days in 1932. They drew the Gweek River and hounds hunted on a nice drag up-stream and put an otter down, but the place was so strewn with large rocks and boulders that he was able to elude us by getting "in" and we dislodged him in rather a curious way the first time he did it. The place was too small for the terrier and we were sitting round discussing the chances when a herculean man was observed to join the group who turned out to be the champion Wrestler of Cornwall. I have always found that strong men are never so happy as when giving an exhibition of their strength, and a few audible whispers, suggesting that had I been younger I should have found no difficulty in dislodging such a pebble, caused him to roll up his sleeves, demand a crowbar and get to work. By alternate banging, swearing and levering he startled the occupant—who was not used to this treatment—to such an extent that he bolted.

If hounds take a line straight inland and the

pace improves rapidly it is usually a fox, but Otters have been hunted five miles from a river and for quite long periods in covert, so it is difficult to be sure, and one must be guided by his knowledge of individual hounds and whether they are trustworthy or not. Scent is, of course, uncertain as in Fox hunting, but usually lies best before the dew is off the ground. For this reason hounds used to meet at nine but now the time is 10.30 or 11.

When putting a terrier into a holt, the entrance may be half under water, tho' inside it is sure to be dry, for Otters don't sit in water any more than anyone else.

The Otter's bite is quicker and usually more wounding than that of fox or badger, and he may fasten on to a terrier and drown him; so it is not a good thing to try a young unentered dog here. Mr. Varndell, Master of the Crowhurst has seen a hound dragged under on two occasions, so you can see the otter is a formidable enemy. Curiously enough if taken young he makes a good pet and I knew one that used to travel up here with his owner on the bus from Brighton. They kept him in the house and mostly fed him fish. Every day he was taken down to the Mill Pond at the bottom of the lane and would swim about and play there. I heard that just lately on one of these excursions, he disappeared and has not been seen since—no doubt the call of the wild was too much for him.

CHAPTER FIVE

BADGER DIGGING—CHOICE OF EARTH AND RECON-
NAISSANCE — MANAGEMENT OF TERRIERS —
BAGGING THE BADGER — HUNTING THE
BADGER AT NIGHT—TREATMENT OF
WOUNDS

P EOPLE often complain of how scarce the
Badger has become and the reason is that
he does not go abroad when people are
about; but there are plenty of them in most
parts if one knows where to look.

Before arranging a Dig it is essential to obtain
the permission of the landowner or tenant farmer
and it is wise to get the Hunt servants and terriers
to go too, if they can be spared, for they are
just as busy at this time of year as in the season
because of the young entry in kennel, many
litters of puppies and various routine duties to
be attended to; also the Hunt Terriers will
have plenty of work to do later and it is not
good to give them too much hard work in the
Summer. Some of the settes are so ancient that
they have become almost impregnable and are
better left alone, others are freshly drawn or only
more recently occupied and it is to one of these

one should go, though it is always wise to ask the Hunt if any particular place wants clearing.

After about twenty-five years in this county I have got to know most of the earths, having seen foxes run to ground in many of them and so I know what sort of difficulties are likely to be found.

The digging may be ordinary loam or clay and there may be many rocks, flints or roots of big trees. One can usually overcome these but it is best to avoid sand because the Badger will dig right away from the dogs which may be buried or suffocated in it.

It is sometimes possible, by the use of Tar, Creosote or Paraffin, to "stink out" Badgers from an earth so that they go into a smaller place nearby but I have never done this and have little confidence in it.

In some settes the holes run under a hard seam of chalk, flints or iron stone and this adds enormously to the difficulties and nothing can be done without a pick-axe and even that bounces off the hard surface like a tennis ball. We dug 50ft. one year and 60 the next at Greatham Common near Amberley. It was not deep but there was hard iron stone and all the time Brock was digging away in the soft underneath. We got a large Badger each time and reached home in the small hours.

The most difficult place I know—I shall never go there again—is in the old British encampment at CISSBURY near Worthing; here the flints and chalk are firmly welded in great chunks of cement. I had a Border Terrier to ground here for six and a half hours and she never recovered of it; she was the only dog I lost in twenty-five years.

Fortunately there is plenty of choice in Sussex: either the Hill (or Downs*) with a glorious view of the sea to the south and towards the north a complete panorama of the Weald of Sussex with its fields, commons and woodlands seen in ever decreasing perspective till they merge in the blue haze of the North Downs; or the Weald and the Forest of St. Leonards which are more closed in, but just as beautiful none the less, with the speckled light and shade on the bracken under the trees and the carpet of blue-bells and primroses beneath the hazels in the spring of the year and very possibly a brook below.

If the weather is very hot it is best to choose a cool place such as the north slope of the Downs (or side-hill) where there are usually high beech trees and where the sun hardly ever penetrates. We dug at Lyon's Bank near Steyning one Derby Day and while a number of people were having fainting attacks and heat strokes on Epsom Downs we all kept as cool as a cucumber.

Having chosen the place, a reconnaissance must be made or the farmer or landowner asked to do so. Nothing is worse than to arrive with a large party at the meet, only to find the Badger

*Since I wrote this nearly all the gorses on the Hill have been burned and they look bleak, black and ugly now.

"not at home." It is a mistake to bring a dog on these occasions but if taken he must be tied up at a distance from the earth.

First of all, there is the trade round the earth. If it is used by a number of Badgers—I have taken 5 large Badgers from one earth—there will be a tremendous trade, and sometimes there is a place where the grass is all trodden down—a sort of playground. A look at the various holes may reveal cobwebs and dead leaves which are of course, against habitation, and offal at the mouth of the hole—as I said before—denotes a fox and usually a vixen with cubs.

It is common to see the bedding of dried grass, bracken or blue-bells drawn out to the mouth of the hole, and it is a most encouraging sign. There may be pug marks and those of the Badger are characteristic, and sometimes claw marks or a hair or two to show if fox or badger is present. Rabbit droppings are discouraging but should not interrupt a complete examination of the sette.

If the Badger is at home some of the holes should show freshly drawn earth, though sometimes on the Downs where there is chalk and flint, they look very stale even when in use: they usually descend rapidly and are horizontally oval in shape with a heaped up mound of earth in front. The size and number of these mounds is a sure indication of the difficulties ahead and it may be a twelve-hour job. I know these places and have got back home at three or four in the morning before now. They should never be tackled with less than four first-class terriers and a half dozen diggers.

In giving this advice I cannot help but admit that when I have had a terrier at an earth I have usually put him in, large or small, even if we only had two diggers, including myself. I

PADS AND PAD MARKS OF FOX, BADGER AND OTTER

remember at Trenant, near Looe, putting a dog into an earth with only old Major Peel there to help me, and we got our Badger in three-quarters of an hour—a pure miracle.

Of course, the weather must be right; heavy rain spoils all, and Peter Beckford's advice in

TOO FAT

his "Thoughts on Hunting"—"Take not out your hounds on a very windy or wet day"— should be remembered.

On the appointed day six stalwarts and at least four good terriers, with lunch and beer will be needed. About a quart bottle per man should be the ration and four pints if it is a long day. Too much beer makes a man "short of puff"; malt liquor and obesity going hand in hand, so that sooner or later he will be unable to get his head into the hole. The locals may get bottled on spirits and I have never used any

MALT LIQUOR AND OBESITY GO HAND IN HAND

but once and then we got some Napoleon Brandy from Wiston to revive a Badger that was overcome with the heat. We had dug him in Lyon's Bank above the house and he was so done that one of the party held his head and fed him the Brandy from a spoon and it was remarkable how he took to it!

First aid equipment, water for the dogs, and a sail cloth bag with brass air holes should be taken; and although tools can be borrowed on the spot, it is wiser to take one's own grafter—a sort of spade curved like a gouge—a pick, swab hook, mattock and crowbar, for there is sure to be hard core to go through and thick undergrowth to cut in order to expose the holes.

For transport I had an old bull-nosed Morris with a suitably partitioned and ventilated dog box behind for the more quarrelsome terriers. I usually drove and the groom with two or three more packed in with the dogs, tools, lunch and all, and accommodated themselves as best they might. It is usually best not to have too big a crowd. The landowner or farmer, a keeper or two—and the Hunt servants as I said before, if available—and the local rabbit catchers make a nice party and the sort of people who get in the way and ask silly questions are not needed. In the old days we used to take a large Melton Mowbray veal and ham pie with bread and cheese and beer, but now-a-days each brings his own nose bag, tho' the diggers get free beer. I've carried some rum chaps in my time, and I remember an old Keeper at Ardingly who sported an ear trumpet and a lantern! I had no use for the former, but the latter came in very useful towards 10 p.m. and the tailing and bagging was done by its fitful glow. That was the kind of man to know what was likely to be needed, and no doubt he heard some funny sounds with his machine. It carried me back to 1915 when some of us were invited by the Officer in Charge of Mines in Gallipoli down a shaft he was sinking under the Turks. He showed us a sort of stethoscope for listening to any counter-mining that might be going on and said that he knew exactly what they were doing but they didn't know what he was doing. Funnily enough the Turks touched off theirs first and there was a very loud explosion and we were all knocked flat. Fortunately the force seemed to be directed upwards and when we came out which we were not slow to do, we saw a large new crater just in front of our parapet!

The car should be brought as near to the sette as possible, for though I would not wish to appear pessimistic, there is always the possibility of being benighted on the earth, and on these occasions the head lights come in very useful. Though I must confess, however, it was generally possible to focus the beam almost anywhere except into the hole! But in any case, it is nice to have the car handy for lunch if and when it rains.

On arrival at the sette the terriers not in use must be tied up securely nearby while one is put in (after removing his collar) at once, as talk and work on the top always alarm the inmates and they may dig themselves in and all the trouble be for nothing, and I have, on more than one occasion, had the day's sport spoiled in this way. Also, it is best to stop some of the holes not under direct observation lest he bolt.

However fresh the sette may look it is only the terrier can tell you if anyone is at home; and if it is a very fine day, Brock may be lying out in the bushes. When the terrier is in, let all be still. Perhaps he will come straight on a badger sitting at the mouth of the hole, or maybe he will have to traverse the whole sette before he finds him, in which case it will be useful to have some fellows with ear to the ground, listening. Presently one of them will shout that he hears barking down below or far away—a mute terrier is, evidently, quite useless, except as a Caesar dog at the end—and one can come and form his own opinion. This is always a difficult time, and the dog may go silent for a while if he loses touch with his game or if he is working at a stop* he may only speak from time to time. In any case it is no good digging until the barking is definitely settled in one place or, in other words, until the dog has cornered his badger in an end hole or cul-de-sac. This may take some time in a big sette where there are ovens (large chambers) and many tubes running in all directions and one or two and sometimes three storeys. Having decided to dig, it is usually best to follow the hole where the terrier went in or the nearest hole at which the baying can be heard, unless this is at some considerable distance, when it is

---

*A mound of earth which the badger leaves between himself and the terrier as he digs his way on.

best to dig down over the sound. It is an awful business to crown down through six or eight feet of chalk or flint rubble, and if that is the programme one must determine the long axis of the tube and dig a trench at right angles to it. This trench should be made so as to come down behind the terrier, otherwise it disturbs the party and Brock may charge the dog back into the main earth. This is a very important point and I remember on one occasion digging right down on to the badger and he charged the dog some ten feet or more clean out of the earth, and we had all our work to do over again. It is absolutely essential to keep the trench broad enough for a full grown man to work and clear away the earth as he goes; the sides must be kept vertical and not allowed to taper as the digging proceeds. The discovery of small holes at about the level where one expected to find a large one is an almost certain indication of being at fault, because Badgers never use such places without enlarging them first. Sometimes it is very hard to find the tube and this is usually because one is not deep enough. A spear may help here, but it is a dangerous instrument and may damage the dog.

About this time the terrier may come out— another should be kept hard by to slip in at once—because he has had enough or has been badly bitten or it may be he will take a breath of air and go back at once, but whatever happens there should be no interval while a man goes off

74

into the woods to get another. This is the way to lose the badger and he will take the opportunity to come out of the cul-de-sac and regain the main earth.

But let us assume that all those difficulties have been overcome and that Brock is cornered. Now is the time to give the "finding" terrier a rest and to put in another dog; or if there is absolutely no doubt about the cul-de-sac one may try unentered dogs if the place is suitable, or someone may want to try a young 'un.

It is not a good plan to put two terriers into an earth unless they are accustomed to work together, and even then they must be dog and bitch; in any case I think they tend to hinder each other, tho' it is sometimes a good thing to use two as the badger comes out and if they know each other no harm can come of it, and it is a great comfort to have them while tailing him. To do this one may have to dig a bit off the roof of the hole, or if the hole is shallow it will pay to dig a second hole behind the badger while the dog faces him; thus he may be got with ease and without any hurt to your dog. Tongs or pincers I will not use as I think them a horrid implement. When used they are introduced alongside the terrier and a foot caught in the jaws; then by pulling on the handles and on the terrier's tail (he will have seized his badger by then) the whole lot comes out into the trench where Brock can be bagged with ease.

It should be remarked that no terrier can

possibly draw a full-grown badger from an earth, as he will dig his sharp claws into the side walls and resist all force. It is another matter in a pipe where the walls are smooth. Therefore, if a man says his terrier has drawn a full-grown badger from an earth or sette, it is quite certain that the truth is not in him.

At long last the Badger is seen quite clearly—his face marked with the familiar black and white stripes and gazing at one through his small "boot-button" eyes. He doesn't say a lot; at least not nearly so much as the terrier who keeps up a stream of shrill invective: he makes a

LOOK OUT! HE'S COMING

sort of humming noise like a bumble bee, and looks very uncompromising, evidently holding the view that an Englishman's home is his castle, no matter what the modern bureaucrat may think or say. Well, there he is, and he'll have to be dealt with somehow. It's "seconds out of the ring," the diggers have effaced themselves with becoming modesty and there's plenty of room in the trench. If there is a good Caesar dog handy he will come in useful, but if the dog is not strong and hard, old Brock will cut through him like cheese and charge down the trench and up the side walls.

It is a very comforting thing to have on some strong boots and leggings on these occasions as a pair of slacks gives no confidence at all; at the same time it must be allowed that the Badger won't interfere if he's left alone. If one has a strong hard dog, it may be best to dig over him and tunnel away at the top of the hole until by leaning over one can get Brock by the tail. If the ground is soft it is sometimes convenient to stand on his back as he comes out and get someone else to tail him. There is a variety of ways to do it but if one takes him hold by any other part, let us say the back, as he goes up the wall of the trench, it is absolutely essential to change one's grip at once and take him by the tail, because if he once gets hold there'll be something missing at the finish!

Some years ago, I had a dig in Grinder's with Alfred Petts—at one time first Whipper-in to the

BAGGING THE BADGER

Crawley & Horsham—and when the badger
came out in the trench I stood on his back to
steady him while Alfred went to take him by
the stern. After a time he looked up and said:
"He hasn't got a tail." Nor had he, but we got
him into the bag alright; his tail must have been

sawn off in a trap as the stump was but recently healed.

Having got a firm grip, he is held out at arms length, for he cannot reach round to bite, and duly dropped in the bag which is held open for his reception. Pig Badgers are more active and can bite one unless vigorously and continuously shaken prior to being dropped in the bag.

Bagging the Badger is the greatest fun, tho' sometimes I wonder if the men holding the bag will agree with me; they always look so frightened and often shut the bag before Brock is in it, and when they do this my language is definitely tinged with haemoglobin! But one cannot be too careful what he says on these occasions in case someone takes it up wrong. I well remember how a huntsman was misunderstood one morning's cub-hunting when he was trying to get a young hound into covert. There was a stout important looking lady at the covert side and just as he got opposite to her he cried: "Leu in Placid, old bitch," and, of course, she thought he was referring to her, and you can imagine her looks!

With regard to foxes, I may say that I have handled very few. If I found we were up to one I would take out the terrier and Charlie usually bolted. In any case, when hunting, all that is attended to by the Hunt Staff.

I was asked the other day for rather more explicit and technical details of how to tail a Badger, "just how exactly it should be done,"

79

and I was rather puzzled to reply. I think the best answer is what was said to the young man who asked how he could become Emperor of China, "just wait for a vacancy and snap it up!"

Anyway, it's not always easy, and I've missed more than one in the years.

With the Badger in the bag as a "Fait Accompli" all seems clear enough, but to the novice, some of the early stages of the day's sport must be very confusing: at first he sees a lot of men flat on their faces, and apparently

"LEU IN PLACID, OLD BITCH" see page 79

dead or, with head poked so far down a hole as to make it appear that the owner has been pushed down there, and there's no one to tell him they are only listening in order to locate the terrier;

ANY OBJECTS OF ANTIQUARIAN INTEREST?

and presently he will see a group of men digging desperately in a deep trench with a high parapet. It must have been very puzzling to a little old gent who came up to us one day on the Hill near Shoreham; he was dressed—I suppose suitably—in straw hat with guard, black alpaca jacket, white trousers and shoes, wearing dark glasses, and leading a pug dog. Addressing himself to one of the Stalwarts in the trench, he asked whether he found any Roman coins or other objects of antiquarian interest, to which the latter, after wiping the sweat from his forehead with the back of his hand, and spitting into the trench as an adjunct to thought, replied: "I don't know nauthen about Roman coins, but we do find a lot of 'ard work 'ere!" and this reply seemed to satisfy the little man, who went on his way contented: but it's no answer to the man of a more enquiring turn of mind. He will look more closely and see that as each man falls out he is replaced by another as energetic as himself while nearby are others, in sharp contrast, completely relaxed over their lunch of sandwiches, cheese and beer which each man takes when he can. Well, it's all very difficult, and as time gets on these too become infected with the prevailing enthusiasm and gather together to stare down into the hole, so that nothing can be seen but their posterior elevation and nothing whatever of the hole. This scene accompanied by the sustained chorus of terriers, each one yelling "blue murder" is all that presents itself to the stranger; can anyone wonder that he's puzzled? But relief is at hand, and all made clear by the dramatic appearance, like a Jack-in-the-box, of the man (holding the Badger by the tail) from amidst the throng.

Badgers weigh up to forty pounds, but the largest we took was thirty-seven pounds on the scales.

Badger digging, like all other forms of hunting, is quite uncertain. I have been to the same earth some five or six times in as many years, and the time taken to get our Badger varied from two

THE POSTERIOR ELEVATION OF MANY MEN

to fourteen hours, and then we didn't get him! One need never be deterred by the man—and there nearly always is one—who says "the last time I put a terrier in here he didn't come out for four days." The thing to look at is the amount of work, the number of holes, and whether it runs under big trees, and listen to anyone who can say what the digging is like. If it is a very hard place, and there is no likelihood of getting home before dark, one must be sure that the party is not of the kind that has to go off before the shops shut or to leave when the pubs open. If they are that sort, it's best not to begin at all. I remember having an unsuccessful and very wet day over by Shoreham when at night-fall I and my groom and one other were left to fill in the hole, and the terrier was still in, barking away, and we had to wait and get him out as well!

There's plenty of trouble in it, and although some of the sport will be as easy as pie and everything go well, at other times it will be the very opposite. The Badger may bolt unexpectedly just as one thought to get him, and he will sometimes go into another hole in the same sette, or in a bigger place nearby, and it will take half the night to get him. Then it's not always too easy to take hold of him. I remember at Hartfield, digging in a place where the going was quite good until we came across large boulders. We had two six-foot trenches, meeting between immense rocks beneath a large cherry tree. There was room enough for an army underneath and the dog had the Badger in an end hole, but we couldn't dig on! In the end, one of us was lowered down head first, and was able to tail and draw out the Badger, while someone else attracted his attention from the opposite hole. I remember that one of our dogs was pretty badly bitten, it was raining in torrents, and the pony that had brought the tools, beer, etc., had skipped and so we had to walk home!

I remember another time getting into trouble with the Master after taking the Hunt servants and terriers to a dig at Shoreham. We got back very late, didn't get our Badger and everyone broke out in a rash next day, from contact with a weed which was peculiar to that place. The

The passing of Mr. Pentecost.

Master told me the next time I saw him: "You're a nice chap, you've half-killed the hunt terriers and the Huntsman and Whippers-in have got mange!"

Sometimes one gets a landslide of earth and he must take great care not to have any overhanging banks. It was always said that a party that dug London Wood some years ago, missed one of their number and asked each other if anyone had seen old Pentecost. The matter was never cleared up as no-one knew if he'd been there or not, and he was not the sort of man to make his presence felt, as the only thing remarkable about him was his name.

If the owner or the Hunt want the Badger put down, it should be done at once. I never allow any baiting; the terriers get badly bitten and it is a barbaric performance at best: I may say here that of more than 200 Badgers taken, I never saw one baited in a loose box, tho' I have seen it openly stated in print that it is the common practice.

If it is not convenient to release the Badger on the same day, he should be kept in a loose box overnight, but the doors must be strongly faced with zinc: it is no good giving him food as he won't touch it; he should be given a bowl of water and a pile of straw, and then next morning he can be bagged again and released at the proper place. It is none too easy to bag one on the open floor and the best way in the case of the boar is to put a hay fork round his neck as he faces into the corner and then he can be taken up easily by the tail: but the sow and pigs are not to be captured thus, for having a narrow face, they slip it between the prongs, and the only way to catch them is to go round until a "vacancy occurs and snap it up!" (vide p. 80). It sometimes helps to put a bundle of straw on the floor and the Badger may go into it leaving his tail exposed.

86

Another way of taking a Badger is to hunt him in the open at night when there is a moon: It must be full or nearly so or one sees nothing and is very apt to break his neck, which is a bad thing tho' I've known men recover of it.

A start should be made about 11 p.m., or as soon as the moon is up and the sette be stopped or else guarded by a man with a hard terrier or two. This is done so as to prevent the Badger coming straight back into the earth as soon as found, as the net in the hole is now no longer used as far as I know.

There is no particular sort of "pack" needed for this sport but Michael Williams of Lanarth, Cornwall, used four or five couple of working terriers and a couple and a half of Bassets to give music as the former give a cry at the start and then run nearly mute. He had some good sport and killed about seven or eight Badgers that way in one season. He usually made a circular cast at a little distance round the earth and his pack were very soon laid on and the fun began. I enjoyed the two or three hunts I had with him very much, but could not help thinking it was a young man's occupation, for however suitable and encouraging moonlight may be for love-making, it affords no adequate illumination for fast work on foot, and I found the high banks, often stone faced and with strong growers on top and the thickly wooded dingles below, very obstructive, so that the sound of his horn and the cry of hounds was all that kept me

87

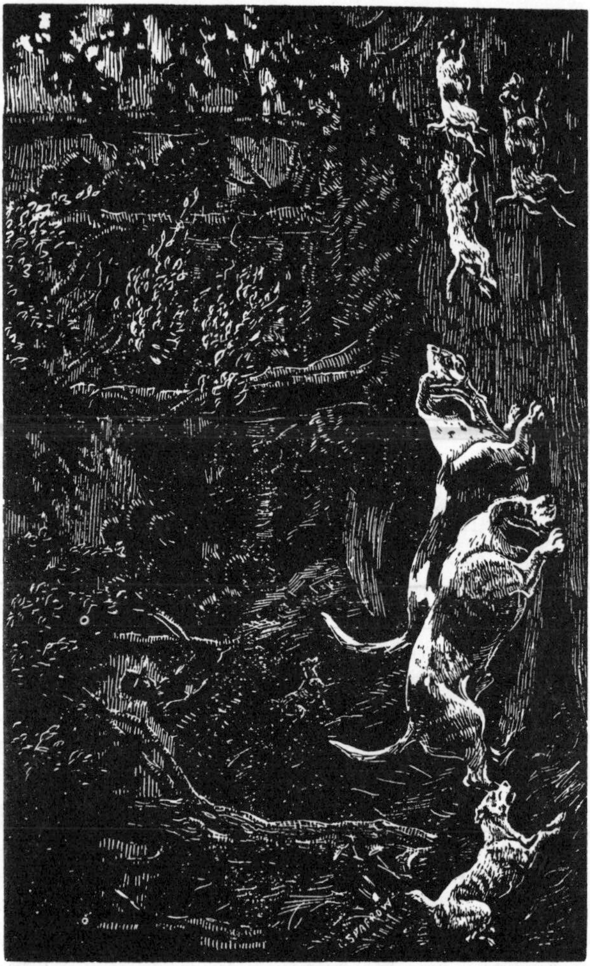

HUNTING THE BADGER AT NIGHT

going. I think he was the best man to take a Badger I ever saw. Neighbours thought him "a very nice gentleman" but terribly noisy at night!

And now, before the finish, a few words of advice on the treatment and dressing of wounds.

A suitable First-Aid Equipment should consist of:—

One pair scissors,
One pair pressure forceps,
Tr. Iodine, 1 ounce,
2½in. bandages—6,
Gauze, Wool.

These should be carried in an air-tight box and not all amongst the lunch! There is rather a difference between the bite of a Fox and of a Badger. The former tends to bite a dog above or through the nose and on the head, making a number of small punctured wounds. The Badger's bite is often more severe and is under the chin or jaw and down the neck. I have seen dogs bitten behind on more than one occasion and they have to be careful when facing the Badger to retreat a little way before turning round to leave the earth. As a general rule the Otter's bite is worse than either.

In wounds of the jaw "TRISMUS" is a complication that must be thought of: it is a rigidity of the jaws caused by spasm of the muscles and is a very dangerous complication. It may be easily fatal but the discovery of Penicillin has improved the terriers' chances very much.

Sometimes a dog will go off his food and in

these cases a teaspoonful of Brand's Essence every two hours will be very helpful.

Wounds are classified as:

(a) punctured
(b) lacerated.

Punctured wounds should be cleaned with a diluted solution of Hydrogen Peroxide in warm water, and subsequently fomented at regular and frequent intervals. They should never be stitched, plugged (except where bleeding is really severe), or bandaged.

Lacerated wounds are not so frequently stitched as formerly. All matted hair should be clipped away, the wound cleansed as directed above, well packed with dry sulphanilamide powder, boric-iodoform, any of the newer M. & B. ointments, and bandaged. Bandages should be firmly but not tightly applied; they may be further protected by elastoplast strapping. A few drops of scent or volatile oil will generally prevent the patient removing the dressing. Where laceration is extensive, bleeding arterial or viscera are involved, only first-aid measures should be adopted until professional attention can be secured.

DISINFECTION

Coal Tar disinfectants should never be used on dogs, either as application or in baths. Control skin parasites by derris in warm soapy water, or by gammexane dust. Wound disinfection by hydrogen peroxide or hypochlorites. Kennels on the other hand, may best be deodorised by solutions of Coal Tar disinfectants in hot water.

CHAPTER SIX

THE WRITINGS OF THE ANCIENTS

IT is both interesting and curious to look back and see what men thought and said hundreds of years ago, and how many of their beliefs have broken down in the light of modern research: and one cannot help forming the opinion that there is one character common to both ancient and modern writers; namely, the habit of copying whole pages from older works and bringing them forward as new, with no check or criticism whatever. Looking at some of the illustrations one cannot help feeling that the artist—to use an expression of our old Master when referring to a drunken servant—"must have seen most of the world through the bottom of a pint mug." And when one sees anything like that in real life it's high time to ask one's friends if they have seen it too. All the same, one finds here and there some lively description and whimsical humour which will repay the trouble of reading some of the more prosy passages. It makes one's mouth water to read what they ate in those early days: "good harness for the throat" and long before rationing and the Ministry of Food.

THE CELEBRATED DOG BILLY KILLING 100 RATS AT THE WESTMINSTER PIT

from an old print

Some of these extracts give an atmosphere of the Regency period which combined luxury and culture with almost barbaric cruelty and I think they will be useful, if for nothing else, in showing what to avoid—how dogs were matched against the Badger and against each other in the pits in big towns and country fairs. Such places were common enough even in Holborn and Westminster and around London.

One of their favourite diversions was to see how many rats a terrier could kill in a given time and that famous dog Billy killed 100 in $7\frac{1}{2}$ minutes and he is seen in the accompanying picture doing his stuff. It's a good enough representation of the event and of the crowd that watched it—was there ever such a "concourse of cads"?

Badger digging is of great antiquity and has been described by many authors. In "La Venerie" by Jacques du Fouilloux (circa 1560) it is shown very clearly that the old squires did the thing in style:

"HUNTING THE FOX AND BADGER, Chap. IX.
How to train the little terriers to hunt Fox and Badger.

"You must understand there are two sorts of Bassets (the word is used here to denote a terrier and not the Basset of to-day) which came from Flanders and Artois; one has crooked legs and is usually short haired, the other has straight legs and is usually rough coated.

"The short legged ones enter the earth more easily than the other sort, and are better for Badgers in that they dwell longer without leaving the earth.

"Those with longer legs have two qualities, they run above ground like hounds and enter the earth with more fury than the others, but do not dwell so long, for the more they strive to get at their Fox or Badger, the sooner they are forced to come out for air. There are good and bad of both sorts.

"Because this kind of hunting is both beautiful and furious and cannot be carried on without great work and trouble, I will here describe how to train and enter the Bassets.

"First they should be entered between the ages of eight and ten months, for if a Basset has not gone to ground before a year old, you will never enter him.

"You must be careful not to treat him roughly at the beginning, lest the Badger or Foxes wound and maim him so that he will not re-enter the earth. For this reason you should never enter Bassets where there are old Badgers or Foxes, until they have been trained or reached the proper age of one year. Also send in an old Basset in front of them to take the brunt of the Badger's attack.

"Seigneurs who wish to hunt with Terriers must be equipped with all things necessary. First a half-dozen strong men to dig, a half-dozen good terriers at least, each furnished with

STRONG MEN TO DIG

ENTERING THE BASSETS

a leather collar three fingers in breadth and furnished with bells, to enter the earths so that the Badgers are the sooner driven into a corner and that the collars protect them.

"As soon as you see the Badgers cornered, or the Bassets becoming tired or short of breath

1561   *Du Fouilloux*
THE SEIGNEUR DOES IT IN STYLE

or the bells full of earth, take up the dogs and remove their collars. . . .

"But to return, the seigneur must have his little cart and when he is in it a young maid of sixteen or seventeen years to stroke his head with her hands.

"He should have half a dozen cloaks to throw on the ground, so that he can hear the baying

of the Bassets. He should have an air mattress. . . .
All the posts of the cart should be hung with
flagons and bottles and at the back there should
be a wooden box full of Indian game fowls,
hams and beef tongues and other good harness
for the throat. If it is winter you must bring a

1575   *Turberville*
GOOD HARNESS FOR THE THROAT

tent and make a fire there to warm yourself or
perhaps 'donner un coup en robbe à la
Nymphe'."
Geo. Turberville   Geo. 1575.

"How to Hunt and Take an Otter, Chap. 74.
"When a huntsman would hunte the Otter,
he should first send foure servants or varlets with
bloodhounds or such houndes as will drawe in
the Lyame*; and let him sende them two up the

---
*Lyame—a lead.

97

river and two downe the river, the one couple of them on that one side, and the other on that other side of the water. And so that you be sure to find if there be an otter in ye quarter: for the otter cannot long abide in ye water. . . . If any of these lyame houndes finde of an otter, let ye huntsman looke in the soft groundes and moyst places to see which way he bent the head, up or downe the river: or if he cannot perceyve it by the markes, he may perseyve it by spraynts and then he may follow his hounde, lodge it even as you would do a Deare, or a Bore. And if he finde not the otter quickly he may then judge that he is gone to couche somewhere further off from the water; for an otter will sometimes seeke his feede a myle (or little less) from his couche and place of rest: and commonly he will rather go up the River than downe for goyng up the streame, the streame bringeth him sent of the fishes that are above him; . . . . You should make a solempne assembly to hear all reportes before you undertake to hunte . . . ., and then he which hath founde of an Otter, or so drawen toward his couche that he can undertake to bringe you unto him, shall cause his houndes to be uncoupled a bowshotte or twayne before he come at the place where he thinketh that the Otter lieth.

"By cause they may skommer and caste about a while until they have cooled their bawling . . . . which all houndes do lightly use at the first uncoupling; then the Varlets of the kennell shall seeke by the rivers side, and beate the banks with theyr houndes until some one of them chance upon the Otter; remember always to set out some upwards and some downe the Streames, and every man his Otter speare or forked Staffe in his hande, to watche his ventes, for that is the chiefe advantage and if they perceyve where the Otter cometh under the water . . . . then shall they watch to see . . . . and strike him with their

from Geo. Turberville. 1575

THE OTTER

speare* or Staffe; and if they misse, then shall they runne up or downe the streame as they see the Otter bend, until they may at last give him a Blowe; for if the houndes be good Otter houndes and perfectly entred, they will come chaunting and trayling alongst by the rivers side, and will beate every tree roote, every holme, every Ozier bedde and tuft of bulrushes; yea sometimes also they will take the ryver and beate it like a water spaniell; so that it shall not be possible for the

*The use of the spear ended about 1860.

Otter to escape . . . . if the houndes be good and that the rivers be not over great."

"The Master of Game of the Grey and his Nature

(Written by Master of Game to Henry IV).

"The grey is a common beast enough and perforce me needeth not to tell of his making, for there be few men that have not seen some of him and also I take none heed to speke much of

Cy papres deulle comment on doit chaseer et prendre le blarian

HOW TO HUNT AND TAKE THE BADGER
The Master of Game (time of Henry IV)

him, for it is no beast that needeth any great mastery to devise of the hunting of him nor to hunt him with strength for a grey flees not but a little way that he is overcome by hounds anon or else he putteth himself into the bay and then he is slayn anon. His most dwelling is in the earth, namely berries, and if he be out thereof he will not walk far thence, he liveth with all vermies and kavies and of all fruits and of all things as the fox but he dare not adventure him so far by day as the fox for he cannot, may not flee. He liveth more by sleeping than by any other thing. Once in the year they farrow as the fox. When they be hunted he defendeth him long and mightily and have evil biting and venemous as the fox and yet he defend him better than the fox. It is a beest of the world that gaderith most greece beareth medecyne as that of the fox and yet well more. Men say that if a child that never had wered shoon and the first shoon that he wore were makyd of the greyes skin that child shuld hele horses of farsyn if he shuld ryde upon him, but thereof make I non affirmacion. His flesh is not to ete nor that of the fox nor of the wolf."

"THE GENTLEMAN'S RECREATION
By Nicholas Cox
(? date: the earliest date on the fly-leaf is 1677)
OF BADGER HUNTING

"A Badger is called by several names, viz, a gray, Brock, Boreson or Bauson and in France

Tausson. The male is called a Badger or Boar-pig: and the female is called a sow . . . .

"There are two kinds of this beast (saith Gesner) one resembling a dog in his feet, and the other a hog in his cloven hoof; they differ too in their snout and colour: for the one resembles the snout of a dog, the other of a swine: the one hath a greyer coat, or whiter than the other, and goeth farther out in seeking of its prey. They differ also in their meat: the one eating flesh and carrion

1561   *Du Fouilloux*

THE FOX AND THE BADGER

102

like a dog, the other roots and fruits like a Hog: both these kinds have been found in Normandy, France and Sicily.

"Mr. Turbeville makes mention of two sorts of Badgers likewise, but in a different manner. For the one (saith he) casteth his fiaunts long like a Fox, and have their residence in Rocks, making their burrowes very deep. The other sort make their burrowes in light ground, and have more variety of cells and chambers than the former. The one of these is called the Badger-Pig and the other the Badger-Whelp: or call one Canine and the other Swinish. . . .

"Badgers when they earth, after by digging they have entered a good depth, for the clearing of the earth out, one of them falleth on the back, and the other layeth earth on the belly, and so taking his hinder feet in his mouth, draweth the belly-laden Badger out of the Hole or Cave; and having disburdened himself, re-enters, and doth the like till all be finished.

"These Badgers be very sleepy, especially in the day time, and seldom stir abroad but in the night; for which cause they are called LUCIFUGAE, avoiders of the light. . . . He hath very sharp teeth, and therefore is accounted a deep biting beast; his back is broad and his legs are longer on the Right side than the Left, and therefore he runneth best when he gets on the side of the hill, or a cart road-way. His forelegs have very sharp nails, bare and apt to dig withall, being five both before and behind, but the hinder very much shorter and covered with hair. . . . If she be hunted abroad with hounds, she biteth them most grievously whenever she lays hold on them. For the prevention thereof, the careful Huntsmen put great broad collars made of Grays skins about their dogs necks. Her manner is to fight on her back, using thereby both her teeth and her nails, and by blowing up her skin after a strange and wonderful manner, she defendeth herself against any blow and teeth of dogs; only a small stroke on her nose will despatch her presently; you may thrash your heart weary on her back, which she values as a matter of nothing.

"In Italy they eat the flesh of Badgers, and so they do in Germany, boiling it with Pears: some have eaten it here in England, but like it not, being of a sweet rankish taste. . . . This subtelty they have, that when they perceive the terriers begin to yearn them, they will stop the hole between the terrier and them; if the Terriers continue baying, they will remove their baggage with them, and go into another apartment or Chamber of the Burrow (for know that some of their houses have half a dozen rooms at least); and so will remove from one to the other, till they can go no further, barricading the way as they go.

"The hunting of a Badger must be after this manner: You must first seek the earths and burrows where he lieth, and in a clear moon-light night go and stop all the holes but one or two, and therein place some sacks fastened with some drawing strings, which may shut him in as soon as he straineth the bag. The sack or bags thus set, cast off your hounds and beat all the groves and hedges and tufts within a mile or two about. What Badgers are abroad, being alarmed by the Dogs, will straight repair to their earths and burrows, and so be taken. Let him that standeth to watch the sacks, stand close, and upon a clear wind, for else the Badger will soon find him, and fly some other way for safety. But if the hounds either encounter him, or undertake the chase before he can get into his earth, he will then stand at bay like a boar, and make most incomparable sport."

Sir Thomas Browne (1605—82) in his
"PSEUDODOXIA EPIDEMICA"
or "Enquiries into many received Tenets" refutes at some length the hypothesis that the Badger's legs are unequal.
"CHAPTER V. THE BADGER.

"That the Brock or Badger hath the legs of one side shorter than of the other, though an ōpinion perhaps not very ancient is yet very general; received not only by Theorists and unexperienced believers, but assented unto by most who have the opportunity to behold and hunt them daily; which notwithstanding upon enquiry I find repugnant unto the three Denominators of Truth, Authority, Sense and Reason.

"For first ALBERTUS MAGNUS speaks dubiously, confessing he could not confirm the variety

BADGER CATCHING

thereof; but ALDROVANDUS plainly affirmeth there can be no such unequality observed, and for my own part, upon indifferent enquiry, I cannot discover this difference, although the regardable side be defined and the brevity by most imputed unto the left. Again it seems no easie affront unto Reason, and generally repugnant unto the course of Nature; for if we survey the total set of Animals, we may in their legs or organs of progression, observe an equality of length, and parity of Numeration: that is, not any to have an odd leg, or the supporters or movers of one side not exactly answered by the other. . . . Lastly the Monstrosity is ill conceived, and with some disadvantage, the shortness being affixed unto the legs of one side which might have been more tolerably placed upon the thwart or diagonal movers. For the progression of quadrupeds being performed PER DIAMETRUM; that is the cross legs moving or resting together, so that two are always in motion; and two in station at the same time; the brevity had been most tolerable in the cross legs; for then the motion and station had been performed by equal legs; whereas herein they are both performed by unequal organs and the imperfection become discoverable at every hand."

"THE NATIONAL SPORTS OF GREAT BRITAIN
by Henry Alken, 1832
Hunting (catching) the Badger.
". . . . This animal is by no means as plentiful

in England as formerly, nor the hunting him so much in vogue. It is a night hunt, by moonlight. The arrangement is to stop all the earths, one or two excepted, whilst the Badger is abroad questing, and to place a sac at the entrance of the holes left unstopped, with its mouth extended, the drawing strings of the mouth of the sac being so contrived as to shut the mouth fast, the strings being strained. The Badger driven to earth will enter the sac, strain the strings, and confine himself. In the meantime, it is necessary for men to be concealed near the earth, in order, on the instant, to secure the prisoner. The traps being thus laid, two or three couple of hounds, or terriers, are thrown off, at the distance of about half or three-quarters of a mile from the earths. These start and drive home the game, which is either caught, or left above ground, for the pursuit of the hounds. The best of this sport is, when the hounds run in upon the Badger, before he can reach his den, when he will stand at bay, like the wild boar, and turning upon his back, his natural position both for offence and defence, he will use his sharp teeth and claws with such vigour and effect, that two or three couple of staunch and fierce dogs will not achieve a conquest over him without retaining many bloody marks of his powers and of his vengeance."

.   .   .   .   .

I have included here an article on Badger Baiting from Henry Alken's "National Sports of Great Britain," partly to show what not to do,

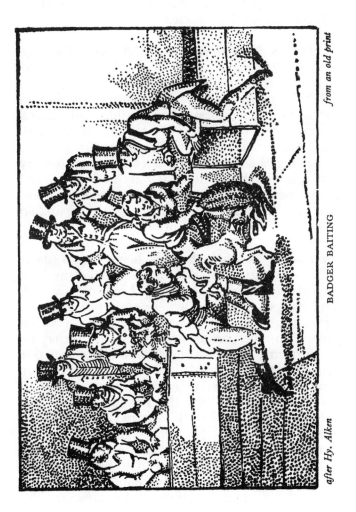

after Hy. Alken   BADGER BAITING   *from an old print* and partly for Henry Alken's illustration which is full of life and character.

"(ALKEN'S NATIONAL SPORTS OF GT. BRITAIN, 1825.)
(2) "BADGER BAITING.

"This most quiet and harmless animal, at the same time possessing invincible and endless courage, has the misfortune to be selected with the Bull, for the pious national English purpose of baiting. Badger-baiting is even yet customary throughout this country, at fairs and races, and in the outskirts of the metropolis at all seasons, as a standing dish of amusement for the dissipated and vulgar of all descriptions, noble, gentle or simple. . . . The instant of opening the door of the Badger's kennel, the dog, being loosed, darts forward with the rapidity of a shot, into the box, the attendant still retaining hold of his tail. The Badger being drawn, one attendant . . . . seizes either the tail or leg of the dog, which he bites with true vermin gripe, ... in order, by the extreme excitement of pain of a superior degree to that afforded by the bite of the badger himself, the fixer may be induced to let go his hold; in the meantime the Badger's WARD lays hold of the tail, while his GEMMAN, keeping an exact account of the time expended by his brother brutes in their contention, prepares to assist in returning the Badger to his box, by taking him by the tail or pole. Re-kennelled, the poor devil of an animal, which, if he possesses the power of wonderment, must indeed wonder what he has done to bring upon himself this repeated torture, is very soon exposed to a fresh attack, and is again drawn and replaced; and this he suffers until the beastly inclinations or cupidity of his torturers and murderers are satisfied.

"The dogs in the highest repute for this sport, are bull-terriers or fixers. The gist of the match, and object of betting are, the number of times the dog will draw the badger from his box, within a given space of time, determined by a stop-watch. . . . As an illustrious example, it is recorded that, within these few years, such a dog drew a fresh strong, and game Badger, seventy-four times in ten minutes."

1561   *Du Fouilloux*

HOW TO PHYSIC THE DOG

APPENDIX

★

ANYONE WITH A working Terrier which does not
conform to the usual shape, and is perhaps of
unknown breeding, is apt to describe him as
"a sort of Jack Russell" and so I thought it
would be of considerable interest to include an
account of the Rev. John Russell's terrier
'Trump.'

EXTRACT *from*
"A MEMOIR OF THE REVD. JOHN RUSSELL"
descriptive of his terrier 'TRUMP' 1878.

"Before he had reached Marston, a milkman
met him with a terrier—such an animal as
Russell had as yet only seen in his dreams; . . .
he never budged from the spot till he had won
the prize and secured it for his own. She was
called 'TRUMP', and became the progenitress of
that famous race of terriers which, from that
day to the present, have been associated with
Russell's name at home and abroad. . . An oil
painting of 'Trump' is still extant at Tordown. . .
I will try, however imperfectly, to describe the
portrait as it now lies before me. (She was
bought in 1814).

"In the first place, the colour is white with
just a patch of dark tan over each eye and ear,
while a similar dot, not larger than a penny

piece, marks the root of the tail. The coat, which is thick, close and a trifle wiry, is well calculated to protect the body from wet and cold, but has no affinity with the long, rough jacket of a Scotch terrier. The legs are straight as arrows, the feet perfect; the loins and conformation of the whole frame indicative of hardihood and endurance; while the size and height of the animal may be compared to that of a full-grown vixen fox.

" 'I seldom or ever see a real Fox Terrier nowadays,' said Russell recently to a friend who was inspecting a dog show containing a hundred and fifty entries under that denomination; 'they have so intermingled strange blood with the real article that, if he were not informed, it would puzzle Professor Bell himself to discover what race the so-called fox terrier belongs to. . .'

"Hence, well may Russell be proud of the pure pedigree he has so long possessed and so carefully watched over. Tartars they are, and ever have been, beyond all doubt; going up to their fox in any earth, facing him alternately with hard words and harder nips, until at length he is forced to quit his stronghold, and trust to the open for better security.

"A fox thus bolted is rarely a pin the worse for the skirmish; he has had fair play given him, and instead of being half strangled, is fit to flee for his life. The hounds, too, have their chance, and the field are not baulked of their expected run.

"Russell's country is technically known as

a hollow one; that is, a country in which rocky fastnesses and earths, excavated by badgers, abound in every direction. Consequently, in every hunting day, a terrier or two invariably accompanied him to the field; and certainly no general ever depended with more trust on the services of an aide-de-camp that he on those of his terriers. If in chase they could not always live with the pack, still they stuck to the line, and were sure to be there or thereabouts when they were wanted, if the hounds threw up even for a minute.

"'I like them to throw their tongue freely when face to face with their enemy,' said Russell one day, as he stood listening to his famous dog 'Tip' marking energetically in a long drain some six feet below the surface; 'you know then where they are, and what they're about.'

"Entered early, and only at fox, Russell's terriers were as steady from riot as the staunchest of his hounds, so that, running together with them, and never passing over an earth without drawing it, they gave a fox, whether above ground or below it, but a poor chance of not being found, either by one or the other. A squeak from a terrier was the sure signal for a find, and there was not a hound in the pack that would not fly to it, as eagerly as to Russell's horn, or his own wild and marvellous scream."

BIBLIOGRAPHY

★

THE BOOK OF ST. ALBANS   *by Dame Juliana Berners* 1406

A TREATISSE OF ENGLISHE DOGGES   *by Dr. Cains* 1576

"THE MASTER OF GAME"   *(Temp. Henry IV)*

"LA VENERIE"   *by Jacques Du Fouilloux*

THE NOBLE ART OF VENERIE OR HUNTING
     by George Turberville 1575

THE GENTLEMAN'S RECREATION   *by Nicholas Cox*

THE GENTLEMAN'S RECREATION   *by Richard Blome*

PSEUDODOXIA EPIDEMICA   *by Sir Thomas Brown* 1605–82

RURAL SPORTS   *by Revd. Wm. B. Daniel* 1801

SPORTSMAN'S CABINET   *Anonymous* 1804

SPORTS AND PASTIMES OF THE ENGLISH   *by Strutt*

NATIONAL SPORTS OF GREAT BRITAIN   *by Henry Alken* 1832

A MEMOIR OF THE REV. JOHN RUSSELL
     originally published in Bailey's Magazine 1878

RECORDS OF THE OLD CHARLTON HUNT
     by the Earl of March 1910

THE TERRIER   *by Rawden Lee* 1889

BEAGLE AND TERRIER   *by Roger Free*

ROD, POLE AND PERCH   *by Cameron, L.C.R.*

HUNT AND WORKING TERRIERS   *Jocelyn Lucas* 1931

Freddie Kerns - Earl's Stopper to Western Hounds

from an old print